How to use this book 

Follow the advice, in italics, where given.
Support the children as they read the text that is shaded in cream.
***Praise** the children at every step!*
Detailed guidance is provided in the Read Write Inc. Phonics Handbook.
Activity 8 (Answer the 'questions to read and answer') only appears in Sets 4–7.

8 reading activities

Children:

1. *Practise reading the speed sounds.*
2. *Read the green and red words for the non-fiction text.*
3. *Listen as you read the introduction.*
4. *Discuss the vocabulary check with you.*
5. *Read the non-fiction text.*
6. *Re-read the non-fiction text and discuss the 'questions to talk about'.*
7. *Re-read the non-fiction text with fluency and expression.*
9. *Practise reading the speed words.*

Speed sounds

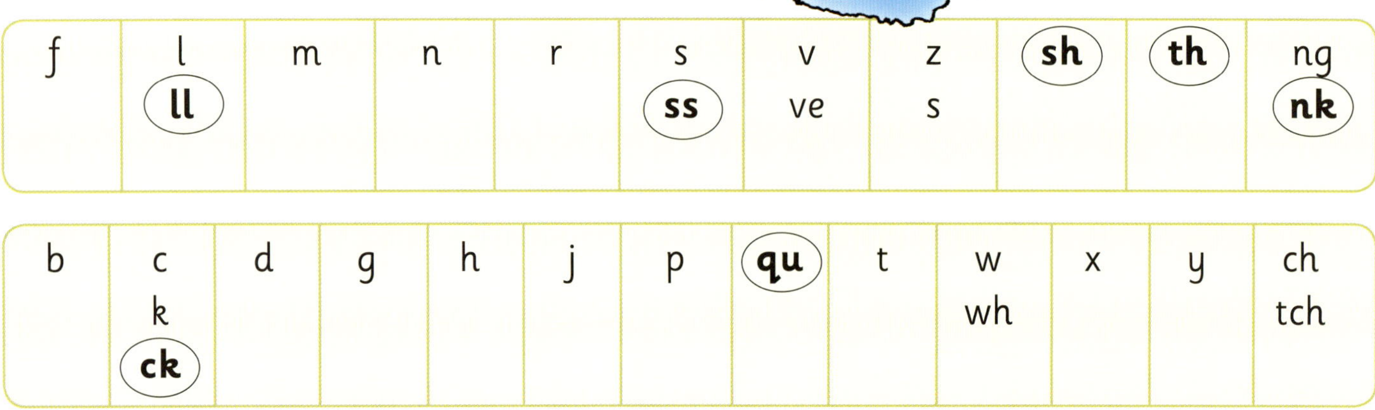

Consonants *Say the pure sounds (do not add 'uh').*

f	l **ll**	m	n	r	s **ss**	v ve	z s	**sh**	**th**	ng **nk**

b	c k **ck**	d	g	h	j	p	**qu**	t	w wh	x	y	ch tch

Vowels *Say the vowel sound and then the word, e.g. 'a', 'at'.*

at	hen	in	on	up	day	see	high	blow	zoo

Each box contains one sound but sometimes more than one grapheme. Focus graphemes are ***circled****.*

Green words

Read in Fred Talk (pure sounds).

gas pond full swim drink trunk

ship flush bath

Read in syllables.

sol\` id → solid li\` quid → liquid an\` i\` mals → animals

a\` cross → across tra\` vel → travel

Read the root word first and then with the ending.

dish → dishes suck → sucking

Red words

what we of be

water elephant* wash*

**red for this book only*

What is it?

Introduction

Have you ever played a guessing game or answered a riddle? This book starts with a riddle and then you learn lots of things about the answer. Good luck with your guess!

Written by Gill Munton

Vocabulary check

Discuss the meaning (as used in the non-fiction text) after the children have read the word.

	definition
liquid	*a liquid is wet and runny e.g. lemonade*
solid	*a solid is hard and keeps its shape e.g. a brick*

I was
he, she, it

Punctuation to note:

It We	*Capital letters that start sentences*
.	*Full stop at the end of each sentence*
?	*Question mark at the end of a question*
!	*Exclamation mark*

It is a liquid.
But it can be a solid.
It can be a gas.
What is it?

It's water!

This pond is full of it.

Animals swim in it.

We can swim in it.

We can travel across it in a ship.

We can wash dishes in it.

We can flush with it.

We can wash in it.
We can have a bath in it.

We can drink it.

Animals can drink it.

This elephant is sucking it up in its trunk.

We can get wet in it!

Questions to talk about 

Re-read the page. Read the question to the children. Tell them whether it is a FIND IT *question or* PROVE IT *question.*

FIND IT	**PROVE IT**
✓ *Turn to the page*	✓ *Turn to the page*
✓ *Read the question*	✓ *Read the question*
✓ *Find the answer*	✓ *Find your evidence*
	✓ *Explain why*

Page 9:	PROVE IT	*As well as a gas, what else can water be?*
Page 11:	FIND IT	*As well as swimming, how can we travel across water?*
Pages 12–13:	PROVE IT	*Why is water useful?*
Pages 14–15:	PROVE IT	*Why else is water useful?*

Speed words

Children practise reading the words across the rows, down the columns and in and out of order clearly and quickly.

dish	pond	flush	solid	across
gas	swim	can	travel	suck
full	wet	bath	drink	but
ship	trunk	liquid	animal	this